A World of Wonders

Geographic Travels in Verse and Rhyme

by J. Patrick Lewis

pictures by Alison Jay

Dial Books for Young Readers New York

Published by Dial Books for Young Readers
A division of Penguin Putnam Inc.
345 Hudson Street
New York, New York 10014

Text copyright © 2002 by J. Patrick Lewis
Pictures copyright © 2002 by Alison Jay
Designed by Lily Malcom
Text set in Mrs Eaves Roman
Printed in Hong Kong on acid-free paper

1 3 5 7 9 10 8 6 4 2

Library of Congress Cataloging-in-Publication Data
Lewis, J. Patrick.
A world of wonders : geographic travels in verse and rhyme /
by J. Patrick Lewis ; pictures by Alison Jay.
p. cm.
ISBN 0-8037-2579-5
1. Geography—Juvenile poetry. 2. Voyages and travels—Juvenile poetry.
3. Discoveries in geography—Juvenile poetry. 4. Children's poetry, American.
[1. Geography—Poetry. 2. Voyages and travels—Poetry. 3. Discoveries in
geography—Poetry. 4. American poetry.] I. Jay, Alison, ill. II. Title.
PS3562.E9465 G4 2002
811'.54—dc21   00-045181

The art was created using Alkyd oil paint on paper with crackling varnish.

For Leigh Ann and Serdar—again and always
J.P.L.

For my parents, Maureen and John
A.J.

Places and Names:
A Traveler's Guide

So many places have fabulous names,
Like Fried, North Dakota,
The Court of St. James,
Siberia, Nigeria, Elyria, Peru,
The White Nile, Black Sea,
And Kalamazoo!
The Great Wall of China, South Pole and Loch Ness,
And 104 Fairview—that's *my* address!

Thousands of spaces are places to be—
Discover the World of GE-OG-RA-PHY!

Travel by boat or by car or by plane
To visit East Africa, Singapore, Spain.
Go by yourself or invite a good friend,
But traveling by poem is what *I* recommend.

Christopher Columbus

Spain dispatched three ships
Across the Atlantic on a
Navigator's hopeless dream of
Traveling westward to Asia.
All dreams end in surprise.

Morning, October 12, 1492:
Ahoy! In the Bahamas, he had
Reached the wilder shores of
Inhabitation, lost in the future,
Anchored at the far end of destiny.

Ferdinand Magellan

Portuguese–born Spanish explorer
First person to circumnavigate the globe
1480–1521

To sail around the world—
That was Magellan's quest!
To bend the compass east
By navigating west.

The Americas loomed there,
So did Magellan's fame.
He crossed the southern tip
Through straits that bear his name.

Into the blue Pacific,
His sailing ships were bound
To find conclusive proof
That Earth indeed is round.

Who Ordered the Sandwich Islands?

Explored and named in 1788
by Captain James Cook

It seems the Earl of Sandwich took,
    While breakfasting in bed,
To eating meat between a first
    And second slice of bread.

The Captain named these islands
    After this quite famous chap.
Across the ocean, Cook would spread
    The word "**SANDWICH**" on the map.

But natives never understood
    The reason why oh why he
Decided that their home should be called
    SANDWICH?!—

        not HAWAII!

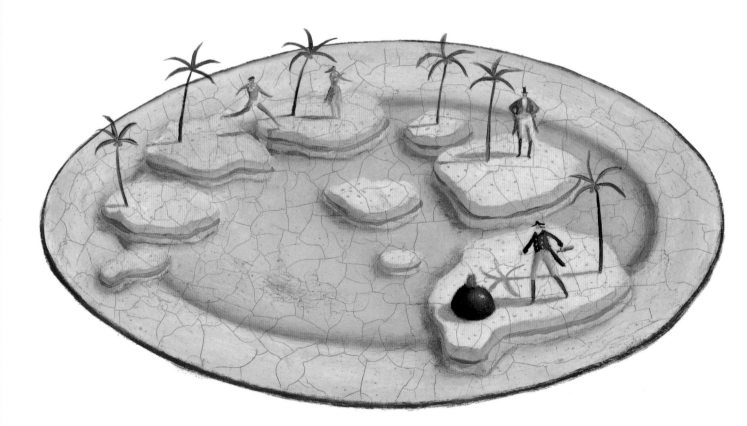

Is the Yellow Sea Yellow?

Is the Yellow Sea yellow?
Is the Red Sea red?
Is the Black Sea black?
Is the Dead Sea dead?

Yes, because there's too much loess—
A fine, rich yellow silt.

Yes, because the red seaweed
Is floating like a quilt.

No, the black comes from,
They say, dark, brooding storms.

Yes, it's dead. No fish, no plants,
Or any of life's forms.
It's no one's fault . . .
Just too much salt!

Marco Polo, Pilgrim

Italian explorer
1254–1324

Journeyed Eastward! China, Ceylon,
Japan, Tibet. Met Kublai Khan.

Sought foreign shores,
sailed distant seas!
And all we knew for centuries

Depended on this lad who wore
The cloak of an ambassador.

Out of the west brave Marco went—
A pilgrim in the Orient.

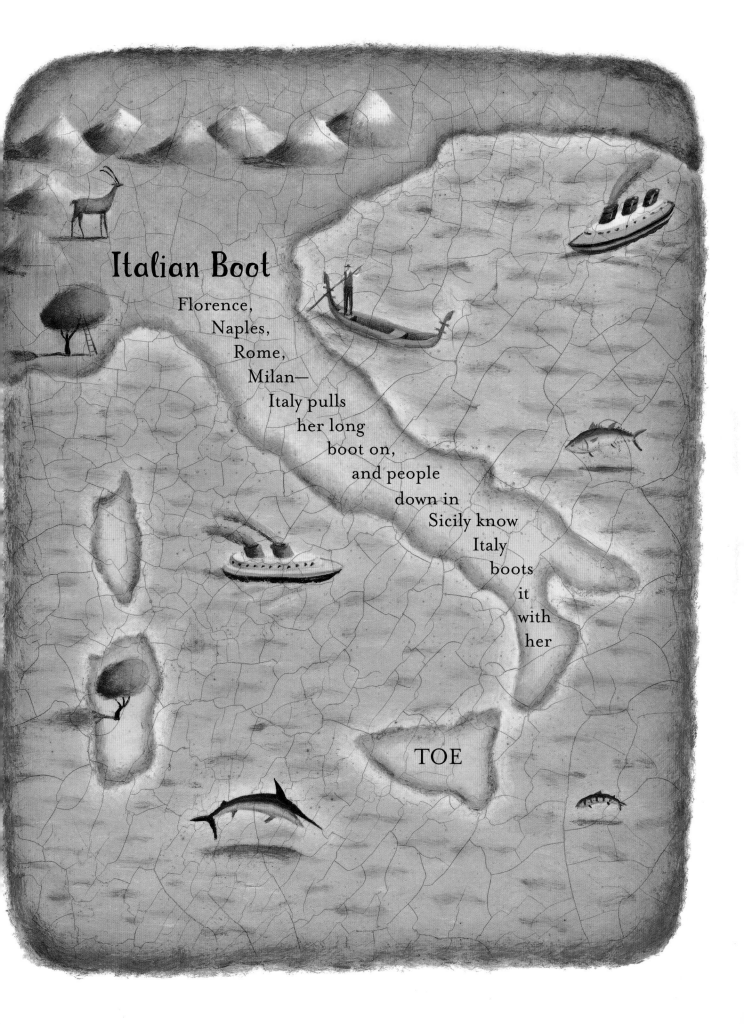

Italian Boot

Florence,
Naples,
Rome,
Milan—
Italy pulls
her long
boot on,
and people
down in
Sicily know
Italy
boots
it
with
her

TOE

Two Animals Talking

The Beetle said, "All Humankind
    Must feel a little smug."

"The Earth has felt the ways of Man!"
    Said Boy. "Now Beetle Bug,
Behold all we have conquered, and
    The continents we've crossed!"

"But since you always win," said Beetle,
    "What have others lost?"

Aurora Borealis

When sunlight dances
down the sky
to take the evening air,

we sit and watch
as clouds go by
in colored thunderwear!

Alaska has
a ringside seat
for taking in the sights,

all lemon-yellows,
greens and reds,
no cloudy grays or whites,

as Mother Nature
now presents—
"The Dancing Northern Lights"!

Who Could Somersault
The San Andreas Fault?

No one could possibly pole-vault
Or trampoline or somersault
Across the San Andreas fault.

The one unlucky lad who tried—
From Malibu to Riverside—
Could feel the continent divide!

600 miles long and 20 deep—
Now that is something of a leap.
I think *I'll* stay in bed and sleep.

Anyway, the
road signs
warn ya:

NO JUMPING
OVER
CALIFORNIA!

How a Cave Will Behave

Take a look at these cone-like formations,
And remember, wherever they're found,

A stalactite drips down from the ceiling.

A stalagmite grows up from the ground.

How to Tell Latitude from Longitude

Lines of latitude
Have a flatitude.

Longitudinal lines
Rise like porcupines.

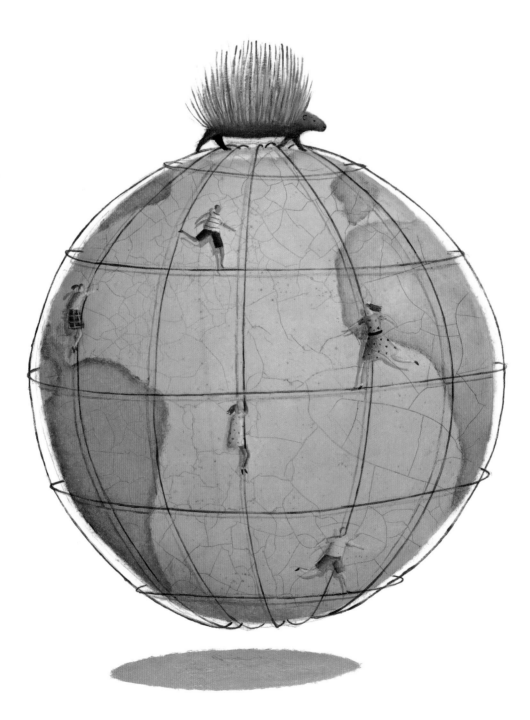

Angel Falls

Venezuela
3,212 feet tall

At least three times higher than the Eiffel Tower stands the world's tallest thunder-shower!

On Top of the World

Edmund Hillary and Tenzing Norgay
First men to climb Mount Everest
The Himalayas
29,028 feet, May 29, 1953

Five miles from earth, they set up camp.
A vicious wind tore at their tent.
They ate sardines, drank melted snow
Before they made the last ascent.

Exhausted, short of breath, the men
Climbed up the final razor wall.
On top now, looking down, they saw

India,

Tibet,

Sikkim,

Nepal!

And Tenzing raised four flags
for they had conquered

Everest after all.

The Arctic and Antarctica: Which is Colder?

The Arctic is *water* all covered with ice.
Antarctica? *Land* (frozen paradise).

The Arctic is up; Antarctica's down—
At least if you reckon from my side of town.

Nobody could live in the Arctic because
It's freezing! (Except maybe Santa Claus?)

Antarctica is even chillier than that,
According to the icicled thermostat.

Why? Because land becomes colder than water.
(But penguins that live there don't want it much hotter.)

136°F in the Shade

Al Aziziyah, Libya
September 13, 1922

Good folks in Al Aziziyah
(Unless they have amnesia)
Remember how in '22
The sun turned up the heat a few
Degrees. And now the record stands:
It's one of Earth's great frying pans!

One Square Foot
Per Person, Please

Did you know that all the people
in the world could stand shoulder
to shoulder in a space the size
of the Indonesian island of Bali?

And if they did?
How jolly!

Did You Know . . .

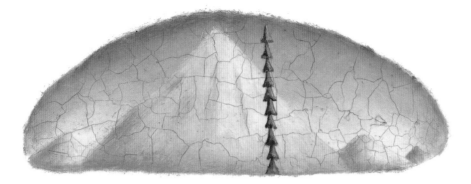

27 Eiffel Towers and Mount Everest are equally tall?
Of the seven continents, Asia is the biggest of all?

The Sahara Desert equals the size of the United States?
Earth is floating on enormous 40-foot-thick plates?

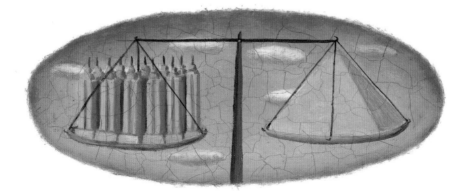

16 Empire State Buildings and the Great Pyramid weigh the same?
A place called Taumatawhakatangihangakoauauotamateaturi-
pukakapikimaungahoronukupokaiwhenuakitanatahu, North Island,
New Zealand has the longest place-name?

The CIRCLE and the POLES

"I'm THE CIRCLE," said Equator,
"An imaginary line.
I circle round the planet
Like a horizontal spine."

"You're THE CIRCLE?" said the North Pole.
"I'm stuck up here in ice,
But if we could get together, CIRCLE,
Wouldn't that be nice?"

So Equator checked the reading
On his thermostat control.
"Let us make some Baked Alaska!"
Said THE CIRCLE to North Pole.

But the South Pole interrupted them.
"While you two shoot the breeze,
I should mention that I'm getting
Slightly warmer by degrees."

"You are?!" THE CIRCLE said to him.
"How about a glacier melt!"
The South Pole glared. Equator flared,
Adjusting his sunbelt.

So the tropics stayed on "simmer"
As Equator let off steam,
And the Poles remained like continental
Plates of white ice cream.

The European City Song

Every heiress goes to Paris—
  Fancy Frenchy Fashion Eden!
I declare the air in Stockholm
  Is the sweetest scent in Sweden.
Take a picture in Pamplona
  Of the running of the bulls.
And in Glasgow, thank the Scottish
For the whimsically oddish
  Highland kilts in tartan wools.

Get together in the Nether-
  Lands beside the Amster Dam!
If you'd like to bike to Zurich,
  Stop for lunch—Swiss cheese and ham.
Oh, the Finns are fine in Helsinki.
  And you will have some fun
Scandinavigating Norway—
Visit Oslo, door by doorway—
  See the setting midnight sun.

Then be open to a Copen-
  hagen Danish walkabout.
Meet your relatives in Brussels,
  Kiss their little Brussels sprout.
European cities offer
  You the perfect picture show
That will tantalize and tickle,
But it puts you in a pickle
  Just deciding where to go!

City Riddles

Where are you if . . .

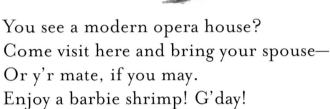

You can cross the Golden Gate,
Find the nation's crookedest street,
Fisherman's Wharf, Ghirardelli Square,
And lots of five-star places to eat?

(San Francisco)

You see a modern opera house?
Come visit here and bring your spouse—
Or y'r mate, if you may.
Enjoy a barbie shrimp! G'day!

(Sydney)

You can find gold onion domes,
St. Basil's Church along Red Square,
A subway people call the Metro?
Mr. Lenin's buried there.

(Moscow)

Someone bows to you politely,
You can ride a bullet train,
Use chopsticks to eat your sushi
In this place where Emperors reign?

(Tokyo)

You think you'd like to loop the Loop,
Or see the Cubs or White Sox win,
Get blown about this Windy City
By the great Lake Michigan?

(Chicago)

You can walk along the Great Wall,
Spend your yuan instead of dollars,
See more bicycles than cars
And lots of folks in Mandarin collars?

(Beijing)

Oceans Five

In waters where bold sailors sail,
Clams clam up, blue whales wail,
This wild wet show, to be specific,
Is the rhythm of the blue Pacific.

On the other side, there's old Atlantic,
Unfathomable and *so* gigantic!
The Arctic Ocean? I'd equate her
To a freezer/ 'frigerator.

And farther south, there's Indian O.
Where rains still reign
and monsoons blow
Toward the southern sea of snow—

The Antarctic, ocean number five,
Where penguins bump and belly-dive
In bathing suits of white and black
Amid icebergs that creak, creak . . .

c r a c k.

Island Hopping

This Archie fellow that I know
Lived on an archi-pel-ago
(An island chain to you and me,
who know about geography).

He hopped around it for a year
As if he were a buccaneer,
Not knowing an archi-pela-goes
Whenever a volcano blows!

So Archie headed for the highlands
As waves rose up and drowned the islands
Until the rock he stood upon
Was archipelago-
                    ing,
                        . . . gone!

Knockabout and Knockaboom

Mohave Desert
Southwestern United States

The wind that whistles desert songs
    By spinning tops of sand
Leaves behind a silent sea
    Of dune-upon-dune land.

The Land of Sand turns hot as fire,
    But once or twice a year
Into the picture of a sky
    Two thunderclouds appear.

They knockabout and knockaboom
To make a THUNDERSHOWER!
And when they leave, they always leave
At least . . . one desert flower.

New Names, Old Places

Sri Lanka used to be Ceylon.
Ancient Persia? Now Iran.

Zaire was Congo way back when,
Now it's Congo once again.

China? Can you guess? Cathay.
That's what people used to say.

Thailand once was known as Siam.
Gold Coast turned to Ghana. I am

Always interested in telling
How a country changed its spelling.

Dutch East Indies? Indonesia!
Once Zimbabwe was Rhodesia.

Burma changed to Myanmar.
Russia, once USSR,

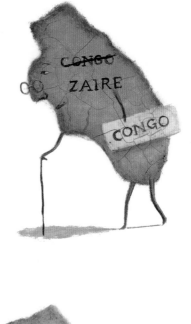

Was even earlier called Rus'.
Other countries introduce

Brand-new names occasionally.
Can *you* find one or two . . . or three?

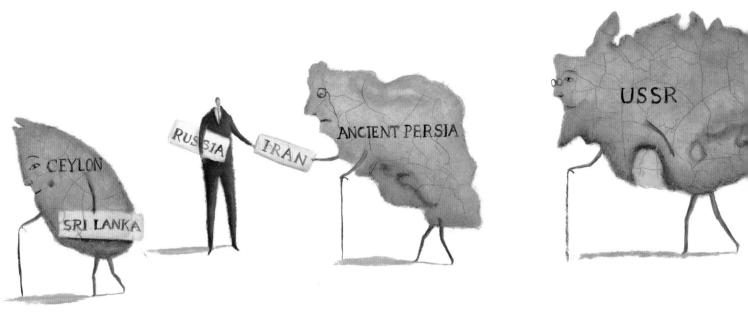

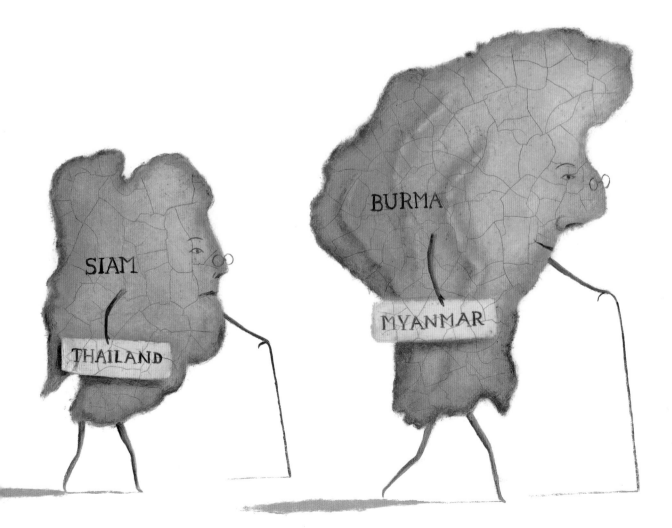

Walk Lightly

Make the Earth your companion.
 Walk lightly on it, as other creatures do.
Let the Sky paint her beauty—she is always
 watching over you.
Learn from the Sea how to face harsh forces.
Let the River remind you that everything will pass.
Let the Lake instruct you in stillness.
Let the Mountain teach you grandeur.
Make the Woodland your house of peace.
Make the Rainforest your house of hope.

Meet the Wetland on twilight ground.
Save some small piece of Grassland for a red kite
    on a windy day.
Watch the Icecaps glisten with crystal majesty.
Hear the Desert whisper hush to eternity.
Let the Town bring you togetherness.
Make the Earth your companion.
    Walk lightly on it, as other creatures do.